New Vanguard • 135

Imperial Japanese Navy Submarines 1941–45

Mark Stille · Illustrated by Tony Bryan

First published in Great Britain in 2007 by Osprey Publishing,
Midland House, West Way, Botley, Oxford OX2 0PH, UK
443 Park Avenue South, New York, NY 10016, USA
E-mail: info@ospreypublishing.com

A CIP catalog record for this book is available from the British Library

ISBN: 978 1 84603 090 1

Page layout by Melissa Orrom Swan, Oxford
Index by Peter Rea
Typeset in Helvetica Neue and ITC New Baskerville
Originated by PPS Grasmere Ltd, Leeds, UK
Printed in China through Worldprint Ltd.

07 08 09 10 11   10 9 8 7 6 5 4 3 2 1

For a catalog of all books published by Osprey Military and Aviation
please contact:

NORTH AMERICA
Osprey Direct, c/o Random House Distribution Center, 400 Hahn Road,
Westminster, MD 21157
E-mail: info@ospreydirect.com

ALL OTHER REGIONS
Osprey Direct UK, P.O. Box 140 Wellingborough, Northants, NN8 2FA, UK
E-mail: info@ospreydirect.co.uk

www.ospreypublishing.com

Author's note

Many people have contributed to the production of this book. I would like to
give special thanks to the staff of the Kure Maritime Museum for their patience
and assistance in permitting me to access Imperial Navy photographs from
the incomparable Fukui Collection. Thanks go out again to Tohru Kizu,
editor-in-chief of Ships of the World magazine, for his kind permission
to use many photographs from his magazine that appear in this book.
Mr Robert Albon provided crucial assistance by translating key material
and helping me to work with the Japanese institutions mentioned above.
As usual, the staff of the US Naval Historical Center proved very helpful.

IMPERIAL JAPANESE NAVY SUBMARINES OF WORLD WAR II 1941–45

ORIGINS

At the start of the Pacific War, the Imperial Japanese Navy had an impressive submarine force of 64 units. During the war, it commissioned another 126 large submarines. Nevertheless, the return on this investment for the Japanese was meager. This book tells the story of the development of the Imperial Navy's submarine force and its wartime exploits. Because of space constraints, it covers only the mainstay submarines of the Imperial Navy, the I and RO classes, and only those that saw active service during the war. The Imperial Navy's midget submarines, its small transport submarines, and a number of German and Italian submarines used by the Imperial Navy late in the war are not discussed.

Birth and growth of the Imperial Navy's submarine force
The Imperial Navy's interest in submarines dates back to 1904. The first Japanese undersea craft were five *Holland* class submarines built by the American Electric Boat Company. Soon thereafter, two additional boats were built to the same design in Japan. The Japanese submarine force continued to expand through the direct purchase of a number of units from Great Britain and France, complemented by licensed production of British and Italian designs.

As part of Japan's involvement in World War I, it received seven ex-German U-boats as reparations. In the area of submarine technology, the Germans were the standard-bearers of the day. The seven boats were studied intensely and provided the basis for the subsequent growth of the Imperial Navy's submarine force. In addition to the seven boats, several hundred German submarine designers, technicians, and former U-boat officers were brought to Japan under contract. However, by 1928, the German presence had dwindled, and the Japanese had become fully proficient in the design and construction of submarines.

World War I had shown the Japanese that the submarine was a key component of sea power. In particular, the Germans had demonstrated

KD2 Type I-52, together with the KD1 Type boat I-51, was one of the prototypes for the Imperial Navy's long-range submarines. The large size and hull design gave excellent seakeeping characteristics. I-52 served briefly during the war before being removed from service. (Kure Maritime Museum)

that the submarine was an ideal weapon as a commerce raider. Nevertheless, the Imperial Navy's General Staff was more drawn to its potential use as an adjunct to the main battle fleet. Initially the Imperial Navy's submarine force was used as a defensive weapon focusing against the US fleet after it entered the western Pacific. In 1920 the first Submarine School was established in Kure, which greatly increased the level of training force-wide. Another important event was the arrival of Rear Admiral Suetsugu Nobumasa to command the First Submarine Division. He greatly improved the rigor and realism of training and began to devise tactics which would fold the submarine force into the Imperial Navy's overall attrition strategy against the US Navy. Construction of new submarines was molded to support his vision of far-ranging offensive submarines.

Following World War I, Japanese submarine construction emphasized large boats with great speed and range. The first large fleet type (*kaigun-dai*, abbreviated as *kaidai*) was based on a British design and could make 20 knots (37km/h) on the surface with a remarkable range of 20,000 miles (32,187km). However, this design was less than satisfactory due to engine problems and the Japanese turned to German submarine technology. Based on the German U-139, the *Kaidai* Type 2 (KD2) was launched in 1922. This design was successful, and served as the prototype for the Imperial Navy's concept of a series of fleet submarines built up until World War II.

Under a system established in 1924, Japanese submarines were placed into three classes. This was denoted by the first three Romanized letters in traditional Japanese syllabary – I, RO, and HA. I-boats were first class or fleet submarines, RO-boats were second class, somewhat smaller submarines, and HA boats were coastal units or midget submarines possessing limited range and displacement. Submarines were no longer numbered sequentially, but within the various types. After the outbreak of war, on May 20, 1942 a "1" was added in front of each boat's number. Later, new boats took the original numbers created by this measure.

The Japanese developed several types of I-boats. Generally, all fleet boats required a high surface speed and a large torpedo armament. Deck guns were also carried. Their large size was crucial to produce excellent seakeeping characteristics and, above all, range. In addition to the *kaidai*, there were several other types of I-boats. First was the *junsen* type or ocean-cruising submarine. These were designed for independent operations across the Pacific and Indian oceans. Operational trials of the early I-boats demonstrated that it was not possible to combine the functions of squadron leader, scouting, and raiding into a single hull, as required to support the doctrine of the submarine force. This led to the design of three different types to specialize in each role. A Types were designed as command submarines to coordinate the operations of a

The K6 was the standard Japanese medium submarine of the Pacific War. Though well designed, they suffered heavy losses for meager successes. RO-46 was completed on February 11, 1944, and was sunk by USS *Sea Owl* (SS-405) off Wake Island on April 18, 1945. RO-46 never even reported attacking the enemy. (Kure Maritime Museum)

The port auxiliary engine room on I-14. Despite their large size, habitability on Japanese submarines was largely ignored. This meant that, especially in tropical conditions, on any long deployment Japanese submarine crews tired quickly. (US Naval Historical Center)

squadron of submarines and possessed long-range radio equipment; B Types were maximized as scouting submarines and equipped with float-planes; C Types were designed for attack and had additional torpedo tubes. Later, during the war, D Type submarines were introduced as specially designed transport submarines.

The development of RO boats was largely ignored between the wars and never received much attention from the Navy General Staff. In 1924, the variety of small units then in service were designated RO. Thereafter, aside from a prototype designed in 1933 (see K5 Type, p.41), little was done to build RO boats until war appeared imminent. RO boats were designed for coastal operations and did not possess the range to operate across the distances of the Pacific.

DEVELOPMENT AND OPERATIONAL HISTORY

Doctrine

Between the wars, Japanese naval strategy was underpinned by the conviction that war with the United States was inevitable. When war came, it would feature a westward offensive by the US Navy's battle fleet that would climax in a decisive fleet engagement in the western Pacific. As the US Navy was larger than Japan's, as mandated by the London and Washington Naval Treaties, the Imperial Navy was faced with developing a doctrine and operational plans to contend with a superior enemy. An important part of the Japanese plans to destroy the US fleet was the concept of reducing the strength of the American battle fleet as it transited through the Pacific. The Imperial Navy's submarine force became an important part of this strategy. Accordingly, the Japanese became the leading proponents of large, ocean-going submarines. In order to contribute to the Imperial Navy's decisive battle concept, submarines were tasked to perform extended reconnaissance of the enemy battle fleet (including while in port), shadow and pursue it, and, most importantly, attack and attrite it before the decisive engagement. By 1930, this strategy had become dogma.

Beginning in 1938, the Imperial Navy finally decided to test how its submarine force was able to execute the various tactical aspects of this mission. The results of these exercises revealed how impractical the entire Japanese submarine doctrine was in reality. Two key lessons were

I-68 in 1934 after completion. Later renumbered I-168, I-68 achieved fame during the battle of Midway when she sank the carrier USS *Yorktown* (CV-5) under her skipper, Commander Tanabe Yahachi. Tanabe survived the war, but I-168 was sunk just over a year later by submarine USS *Scamp* (SS-277). (US Naval Historical Center)

This photograph of a C Type boat was taken by American forces on Kwajalein Island in 1944. Despite the streamlining of its class, which improved underwater performance, the large size of the boat is clear. This made the I-boats relatively easy to detect by radar and sonar. (US Naval Historical Center)

the difficulty in conducting close surveillance of well-defended fleet units, and the vulnerability of large submarines to detection. The difficulty of conducting command and control of submarines acting in concert with the battle fleet was also amply demonstrated.

Another disconcerting lesson was the extreme difficulty submarines had in executing the attack phase of their doctrine. The Japanese believed that the best position for a torpedo attack was at a distance of some 1,500 yards (1,372m) off the bow of the target. To achieve such a position, the submarine would have to gain contact on the enemy force and then use its high surface speed to place itself across the enemy's path of movement. Unless the enemy's line of advance could be clearly predicted, a picket line of submarines was deployed across the possible lines of advance. During exercises in 1939 and 1940 it was found that the enemy force usually transited the submarines' operating area unscathed as it was hard enough just to maintain contact with an enemy force, much less to speed ahead and wait submerged for the enemy to come cruising by. Torpedo attacks on the surface were found to be impracticable because of the likelihood of detection.

All of the lessons gained from these prewar exercises had great impact on wartime operations; for example, the emphasis on concealment translated during the war into extreme caution. Overall, the prewar exercises demonstrated the basic unsuitability of Japanese submarine doctrine; however, the Japanese chose to relearn this lesson during the war under the penalty of heavy losses.

Japanese submarine doctrine clearly focused on the enemy's battle fleet at the expense of developing the strategy and tactics required to attack the enemy's commerce and sea lines of communication. Curiously, when Japanese submarines were exercised against merchant targets, they were found to be effective. However, not only was this lesson not heeded with regard to the employment of Japanese submarines, but neither was the converse possibility, that enemy submarines could cripple Japan's seagoing commerce. The Japanese did consider attacks on US shipping to be an important part of a Pacific war, but only if such operations did not interfere with the primary mission of attacking the enemy's battle fleet.

Crewmen of I-58 in her torpedo room after the war. Torpedo technology was the only major area where Japanese submarines had an advantage over their American counterparts. (US Naval Historical Center)

Weapons
The Imperial Navy's torpedoes were renowned for their range and killing power. Contemporary Japanese torpedoes used pure oxygen instead of air,

which gave them excellent range and speed and all but eliminated the conspicuous bubble track that made the torpedo easily visible. Another hallmark was their reliability. Unlike in the US Navy, between the wars the Imperial Navy had thoroughly tested its torpedoes in a number of test shots against target ships. This paid off handsomely during the Pacific War.

The best Japanese submarine torpedo was the 21-in. Type 95, which was designed in 1935 and entered production in 1938, with 2,200 being produced. An updated version (Model 2), introduced in 1943, utilized a shorter oxygen vessel, reducing its maximum range to 8,200 yards (7,500m) but possessed a longer warhead with a larger explosive charge of 1,210lb (550kg).

21-in. (53.3cm) TYPE 95 (1935) TORPEDO SPECIFICATIONS

Weight:	3,671lb (1,665kg)
Length:	23ft 5¼in. (7,150mm)
Explosive charge:	891lb (405kg)
Ranges:	9,850yd at 49–51kt (9000m at 91–94.5km/h)
	13,100yd at 45–47kt (12,000m at 83.5–87km/h)

Not all submarine torpedoes were oxygen propelled. A number of other torpedoes were used including the Type 96 enriched air and the Type 92 electric, and also, during the first part of the war, a number of older torpedoes, which were propelled by a mix of kerosene fuel and compressed air. The most important older torpedo was the Type 89.

21-in. (53.3cm) TYPE 89 (1929) TORPEDO SPECIFICATIONS

Weight:	3,677lb (1,668kg)
Length:	23ft 6in. (7,163mm)
Explosive charge:	661lb (300kg)
Ranges:	6,000yd at 45kt (5,500m at 83.5km/h)
	6,550yd at 43kt (6,000m at 79.5km/h)
	10,900yd at 35kt (10,000m at 65km/h)

In addition to their torpedo armament, almost all I and RO boat classes were equipped with deck guns. These were intended for use against merchant ships in situations where it was not necessary or worth expending a torpedo and for self-defense against escorts. During the war, four different types of deck gun were carried by Imperial Navy submarines. The standard deck gun for larger I-boats was the 5.5-in. gun, which dated from 1922. The Type 88 3.9-in. gun, introduced in 1928, was fitted on board the KD5 boats but did not see widespread service. Most of the KD Type boats carried the larger 4.7-in. gun introduced in 1922. The smallest deck gun entering service was the 3in., which was fitted on some units of the KD6 class and all RO boats.

IMPERIAL NAVY SUBMARINE DECK GUN SPECIFICATIONS

Weapon	Maximum range	Shell weight
11th Year Type 5.5in./40 (14cm):	17,500yd (16,000m)	83.8lb (38kg)
11th Year Type 4.7in./45 (12cm):	17,500yd (16,000m)	45lb (20.4kg)
Type 88 3.9in./50 (10cm):	17,700yd (16,200m)	28.7lb (13kg)
Type 88 3in./40 (8cm):	11,800yd (10,800m)	13.2lb (6kg)

Aircraft

A peculiar aspect of the Imperial Navy's submarine force was its heavy use of aircraft launched from submarines. Other navies experimented with this, but only the Imperial Navy pursued it with such energy. This expanded the scouting range of the submarine and, in theory, permitted the submarine to reconnoiter enemy ships, even in port. Experiments with operating aircraft from submarines began in 1923, and in 1925 the first aircraft was flown off a KRS Type submarine. The first wholly Japanese-designed seaplane to operate from submarines was the E9W1 Submarine Reconnaissance Seaplane, which entered service in 1935.

The most used submarine-launched aircraft in naval history was the E14Y1 (codenamed GLEN by the Allies). The E14Y1 was a low-wing monoplane with two small floats, and possessed a range of 560 miles (900km) and a top speed of 153mph (246km/h). The aircraft remained in production until 1943; 138 were built. Space was provided for two crewmen, a pilot, and an observer. Two 66lb (30kg) bombs could be carried.

The components for the E14Y1 could be stored in the submarine's tight hangar and could be assembled within 15 minutes from the time the submarine surfaced. With experience, the crew could cut this time to just over 6 minutes. Launching was accomplished by a pneumatic catapult. Recovery was performed by landing in the water near the submarine and having a collapsible crane bring the aircraft aboard for it to be dismantled and stowed in the watertight hangar.

Introduced in 1922, the 5.5-in. gun was the standard deck gun on larger I-boats. The gun weighed almost 8½ tons (7.7 tonnes). It was hand-operated and could fire five rounds per minute. (US Naval Historical Center)

The follow-on to the E14Y1 was the M6A1 Seiran floatplane. Built to operate off AM and STo Type boats, the Seiran was intended to be used not in a reconnaissance role, but as an attack aircraft. The project was undertaken in the utmost secrecy as the success of the entire concept depended on surprise. The aircraft would possess sufficient speed to evade interception and sufficient range to strike targets well inland without giving away the location of the launching submarine.

A 3.9-in. gun fitted forward on the KD5 Type submarine I-69. It could be employed against surface targets or as an anti-aircraft weapon, and could fire up to 12 rounds per minute. (*Ships of the World* magazine)

The Seiran was stowed as a whole aircraft. Provisions were made to warm the engine in its hangar while the submarine was submerged. When the host submarine surfaced, the aircraft could be prepared for launch without its floats in 4.5 minutes, with another 2.5 minutes to fit the floats. Weapons load was one 1,874lb (850kg) aircraft torpedo, one 1,764lb (800kg) bomb, or two 551lb (250kg) bombs.

Series production began in 1944, but was hampered by earthquakes and American bombing. By March 1945, production was stopped and only 14 Seirans were delivered. These Seirans were en route to their first target when the war ended.

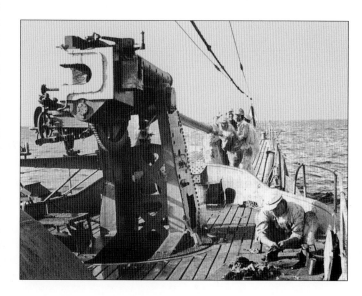

Radar

One of the Imperial Navy's foremost shortcomings during the Pacific War was its failure to develop radar. This had a crippling effect operationally on its submarine force. The lack of an air warning radar on Japanese submarines increased their vulnerability to air attack, especially at night. This was crucial given the already excessive diving times of Japanese submarines. The Type 13 was the standard Japanese air search radar for submarines; however, it was not until April 1944 that this bulky radar was adapted to submarine use. Performance was mediocre, with the capability to detect a group of aircraft at 60 miles (97km) and a single aircraft at 30 miles (48km). To detect Allied radar, Japanese submarines also employed passive measures. The E27/Type 3 radar detector was introduced well before the Japanese fitted radar to submarines; however, its reliability was suspect. Additionally, late-war Japanese submarines had their hulls and conning towers covered by an antiradar hull coating designated "LI."

The standard surface search radar was the Type 22. This set had two horn-shaped antennae, one for transmission and one for receiving. On most submarines, the Type 22 was mounted in front of the conning tower. Performance against a large surface target was reportedly in excess of 21 miles (34km), but was probably much less on a submarine where the set was mounted fairly low to the water.

I SERIES SUBMARINES

KD2 Type

This unit, along with the KD1 Type (I-51, scrapped in 1941), was the prototype for the large I-boat designs which were to become standard for the Imperial Navy's submarine force. The design was based on the German U-139. After completion in May 1925, she was used in a series of exercises to judge the suitability of the *kaidai* type large submarines. Five more planned units were canceled following the Washington Naval Treaty.

Armament: Eight 21-in. torpedo tubes, six bow and two stern; 16 torpedoes; one 4.7in. and one 3in. deck gun.

War service: I-52 began the war assigned to training duties, until removed from service in July 1942. The hulk was scrapped after the war.

KD2 TYPE SPECIFICATIONS

Units in class:	1 (I-52, changed to I-152 on May 20, 1942)
Displacement:	1,500 tons (1,361 tonnes) surfaced; 2,500 tons (2,268 tonnes) submerged
Dimensions:	Length 330ft 9in. (100.8m); Beam 25ft (7.6m); Draft 16ft 9in. (5.1m)
Machinery:	Two diesels with 6,800shp driving two shafts; electric motors with 2,000shp
Speed:	22kt (40.75km/h) surfaced; 10kt (18.5km/h) submerged
Range:	10,000nm at 10kt (18,520km at 18.5km/h) surfaced; 100nm at 4kt (185km at 7.4km/h) submerged
Operating depth:	75ft (23m)
Crew:	60

KRS Type

These boats were designated large submarine-minelayers and were based on the German U-125/UE II class. They were completed in 1927–28 and were the only dedicated submarine minelayers put into service by the Imperial Navy. Up to 42 mines could be carried in the two mine shafts fitted aft of the conning tower. In 1940, all four were fitted with aviation fuel tanks to refuel flying boats. They maintained their minelaying capabilities.

Armament: Four 21-in. bow torpedo tubes; 12 torpedoes; one 5.5-in. deck gun.

War service: During the initial phase of the war all four units were active as minelayers in the East Indies, off the Philippines and off Australia. The mines laid by I-124 sank two merchants; I-124 also scored the only other success of the class when she torpedoed a third freighter. An attempt to use their aviation supply capabilities in May 1942 before the battle of Midway to refuel H8K flying boats from the French Frigate Shoals came to naught. I-123 and I-124 were sunk by Allied surface ships, and the surviving two units were assigned to the training squadron in 1943. I-122 was later sunk in the Sea of Japan by a US submarine.

KRS TYPE SPECIFICATIONS

Units in class:	4 (I-21 to I-24 [later I-121 to I-124])
Displacement:	1,383 tons (1,255 tonnes) surfaced; 1,768 tons (1,604 tonnes) submerged
Dimensions:	Length 279ft 6in. (85.2m); Beam 24ft 6in. (7.5m); Draft 14ft 6in. (4.39m)
Machinery:	Two diesels with 2,400shp driving two shafts; electric motors with 1,100shp
Speed:	14.5kt (26.9km/h) surfaced; 7kt (13km/h) submerged
Range:	10,500nm at 8kt (19,446km at 14.8km/h) surfaced; 40nm at 4.5kt (74km at 8.3km/h) submerged
Operating depth:	200ft (61m)
Crew:	75

J1 Type

These were the first boats of the *junsen* (cruiser) type. As such, they were designed for independent raiding operations or long-range reconnaissance ahead of the battle fleet. To accomplish this they possessed an endurance of 60 days, combined with a high surface speed and a very long range. I-1 conducted a test cruise of 25,000 miles (40,234km), thus validating the class concept, at least from a design standpoint. Three were completed in 1926 and the last in 1929. Overall, the *junsen* type proved to be a limited success. The large hull required for long range gave them excellent seakeeping qualities on the surface, but made for limited maneuverability when submerged, and greatly increased their diving time. In practice during the war, the boats were used not in their intended independent long-range cruiser role, but as normal attack boats. In late 1942, two ships of the class were modified into transports. This entailed the removal of the after 5.5-in. gun, a reduction in the number of torpedo reloads, and provisions for carrying a 46ft (14m) landing craft or cargo rafts.

Armament: Six 21-in. torpedo tubes, four bow and two stern; 20 torpedoes; two 5.5-in. deck guns.

War service: During the initial phase of the war all four units were deployed off Hawaii, where the Japanese hoped the Pearl Harbor raid would force US naval units to sea to be picked off by submarines. The class was also active in the Indian Ocean during early 1942 and later in the Aleutians. At least two of the boats (I-1 and I-3) were modified into transports. All four were turned to supply duties by late 1942 and all were sunk in this capacity. I-3 was destroyed in December 1942 by US PT boats off Guadalcanal; I-4 followed later that same month, destroyed by a US submarine; I-1 was sunk off Guadalcanal in January 1943 by New Zealand surface forces; I-2 survived until April 1944 when she was destroyed by US destroyers. The four submarines accounted for five confirmed merchant ships.

J1 TYPE SPECIFICATIONS

Units in class:	4 (I-1 to I-4)
Displacement:	2,135 tons (1,937 tonnes) surfaced; 2,791 tons (2,532 tonnes) submerged
Dimensions:	Length 320ft (97.5m); Beam 30ft 3in. (9.2m); Draft 16ft 6in. (5m)
Machinery:	Two diesels with 6,000shp driving two shafts; electric motors with 2,600shp
Speed:	18kt (33.3km/h) surfaced; 8kt (14.8km/h) submerged
Range:	24,000nm at 10kt (44,448km at 18.5km/h) surfaced; 60nm at 3kt (111km at 5.6km/h) submerged
Operating depth:	265ft (80m)
Crew:	68

J1M Type

This single-boat class was nearly identical to the J1 Type, but with provision for an aircraft. When completed in 1932, she was the first Japanese submarine designed to handle an aircraft, but these facilities proved unsuccessful in service. The aircraft components were stored in two watertight cylinders fitted port and starboard aft of the conning tower. Sources conflict on whether a catapult was fitted, but photographic evidence suggests that one was provided. However, the hangar arrangement required excessive time to assemble the aircraft and by 1940 the aircraft-handling equipment was replaced by a second 5.5-in. deck gun.

Armament: Six 21-in. bow torpedo tubes and 20 torpedoes; one (later two) 5.5-in. deck guns; one floatplane (until 1940).

War service: I-5 was deployed off Hawaii during the initial stages of the war, but, like almost all of her sister ships, never engaged a target. She was then sent to the Indian Ocean during early 1942, again with no success. Highlights of her 1943 service included supply missions in the Solomons and assisting in the evacuation of the Japanese garrison from Kiska Island in the Aleutians. The boat failed to score a single success before she was sunk off Saipan in the Marianas in July 1944 by US surface ships.

I-2 belonged to the four-boat J1 Type. Note the 5.5-in. deck guns fore and aft of the conning tower and the two retractable radio masts. The J1 Type was obsolescent at the start of the war, but still saw extensive service. I-2 was lost on April 7, 1944 off New Ireland to the destroyer USS *Saufley* (DD-465). (Kure Maritime Museum)

J1M TYPE SPECIFICATIONS

Units in class:	1 (I-5)
Displacement:	2,243 tons (2,039 tonnes) surfaced; 2,921 tons (2,650 tonnes) submerged
Dimensions:	Length 320ft (97.5m); Beam 30ft 3in. (9.2m); Draft 16ft 6in. (5m)
Machinery:	Two diesels with 6,000shp driving two shafts; electric motors with 2,600shp
Speed:	18kt (33.3km/h) surfaced; 8kt (14.8km/h) submerged
Range:	24,000nm at 10kt (44,448km at 18.5km/h) surfaced; 60nm at 3kt (111km at 5.6km/h) submerged
Operating depth:	260ft (79m)
Crew:	80

J2 Type

This single-boat class was generally completed to the same pattern as I-5. This included the awkward aircraft-handling arrangement that launched the aircraft against the boat's forward movement. I-6 was completed in 1935 with more powerful diesel engines that translated into a higher surface speed at the expense of range.

Armament: Six 21-in. torpedo tubes, four bow and two stern, and 17 torpedoes; one 5-in. deck gun, one 13mm machine gun; one floatplane.

War service: I-6 was the most successful of the *junsen* type submarines. On January 11, 1942, 500 miles (805km) southwest of Oahu, she sighted and hit USS *Saratoga* (CV-3) with a Type 89 torpedo. The resulting damage

I-6 was one of the first Japanese submarines equipped to handle aircraft. The two cylinders aft of the conning tower provided stowage. Assembly and recovery of the aircraft were assisted by the crane. I-6 was lost with her crew on June 16, 1944, in a collision with a Japanese merchant ship. (*Ships of the World* magazine)

put the carrier out of the war for six months. When deployed to the Indian Ocean in April 1942, she sank two British merchants. After laying German acoustic mines off Brisbane, Australia, she joined her sister ships in running supplies to New Guinea, making nine runs to Lae. Subsequently, she participated in the evacuation of Kiska and then resumed supply duties in the New Guinea and New Britain area. I-6 was sunk when rammed by a Japanese merchant ship as she surfaced near a Japanese convoy on July 16, 1944.

J2 TYPE SPECIFICATIONS

Units in class:	1 (I-6)
Displacement:	2,243 tons (2,039 tonnes) surfaced; 3,061 tons (2,777 tonnes) submerged
Dimensions:	Length 323ft (98.5m); Beam 29ft 9in. (9m); Draft 17ft 6in. (5.3m)
Machinery:	Two diesels with 8,000shp driving two shafts; electric motors with 2,600shp
Speed:	20kt (37km/h) surfaced; 7.5kt (13.9km/h) submerged
Range:	20,000nm at 10kt (37,040km at 18.5km/h) surfaced; 60nm at 3kt (111km at 5.6km/h) submerged
Operating depth:	265ft (80m)
Crew:	80

J3 Type

These two boats were the largest Japanese submarines built prior to the Pacific War. Though typed as *junsen*, they were developed from the KD3 and KD4 types, as shown by the design of their conning tower. Their great size made them suitable for squadron commander units. In many respects, these were the ultimate development of the cruiser type boat, with a high surface speed, great endurance, and the retention of a floatplane and aircraft facilities. The two units were completed in 1937 and 1938.

Armament: Six 21-in. bow torpedo tubes and 20 torpedoes; one 5.5-in. deck gun, two twin and one single 13mm machine gun; one floatplane. In early 1943, both boats had their twin 13mm mounts replaced by a twin 25mm gun. Also in 1943, I-8 had her single 5.5-in. gun replaced by a twin 5.5-in. mount, the only time a Japanese submarine was fitted with this weapon. In 1944, I-8 had her catapult and hangar removed and was fitted with mountings for four *kaiten*, or suicide torpedoes.

The two J3 boats both proved successful in service. The crew members on deck aft of the conning tower hide the small aircraft hangar and the catapult. I-7 was lost on July 5, 1943, when she was damaged by USS *Monaghan* (DD-354) and then grounded and scuttled off Kiska Island. (Kure Maritime Museum)

I-8, mid-war, with her dual 5.5-in. deck gun mounted forward of her conning tower. This was apparently fitted for her trip to Europe. I-8 was lost on March 31, 1945 off Okinawa to destroyer USS *Morrison* (DD-560), with the loss of all hands. (*Ships of the World* magazine)

War service: Both units were deployed off Hawaii at the start of the war. I-7 launched her E9W1 floatplane to reconnoiter Pearl Harbor on December 17. Later, I-7 was moved into the Indian Ocean where she sank a merchant ship. After sinking another merchant in the Aleutians, I-7 participated in the evacuation of Kiska. She was sunk in July 1943 off Kiska by US destroyers following her last visit. I-8 had a long and varied career. After operating off Hawaii, she was engaged in making supply runs to Guadalcanal. In June 1943, she commenced the second trip by an Imperial Navy submarine to Europe, arriving in Brest, occupied France, on August 31, 1943. She departed on October 5 with a load of German war technology. Her return to Kure on December 21, 1943 completed a voyage of 30,000 miles (48,280km). This was the only successful round-trip voyage by a Japanese submarine during the war. In 1944, her sinking of a Dutch freighter in the Indian Ocean was followed by an atrocity in which 98 crew and passengers were killed on the submarine's deck. Two more British merchants were sunk, and in July 1944, when I-8 sank a US Liberty ship, the massacre of the crew was repeated. I-8 was sunk off Okinawa by US destroyers in March 1945.

J3 TYPE SPECIFICATIONS

Units in class:	2 (I-7, I-8)
Displacement:	2,525 tons (2,291 tonnes) surfaced; 3,583 tons (3,250 tonnes) submerged
Dimensions:	Length 358ft 6in. (109.3m); Beam 29ft 9in. (9m); Draft 17ft 3in. (5.2m)
Machinery:	Two diesels with 11,200shp driving two shafts; electric motors with 2,800shp
Speed:	23kt (42.6km/h) surfaced; 8kt (14.8km/h) submerged
Range:	14,000nm at 16kt (25,928km at 29.6km) surfaced; 60nm at 3kt (111km at 5.6km/h) submerged
Operating depth:	330ft (100m)
Crew:	80

KD3A/B Types

These ships were derived from the KD2 design with a continued emphasis on surface speed and long range. The four KD3A units differed from the five KD3B variants by the shape of their bow and the configuration of their conning sail. These boats were completed between 1927 and 1930 and were reaching the end of their service lives by the onset of war.

Armament: Eight 21-in. bow torpedo tubes and 16 torpedoes; one 4.7-in. deck gun. No aircraft facilities were fitted. In 1945, four boats (I-156, I-157, I-158, and I-159) were fitted to carry two *kaiten*.

War service: I-63 was sunk by collision with I-60 in 1939. The remaining units were very active early in the war, but from March 1942

all surviving boats were assigned as training assets and removed from active duty. The boats were assigned to support the invasion of the Dutch East Indies where they were fairly successful, sinking 18 confirmed ships. One ship, I-58, sighted the Royal Navy's Force Z on December 10 in the South China Sea and launched an unsuccessful torpedo attack. I-60 was sunk in January 1942 by a British destroyer. The remaining units were involved in the Midway operation and later in the Aleutians. After being assigned to training duties, I-153 and I-154 were laid up in January 1944. The other boats continued training duties until the war's end.

KD3A/B TYPE SPECIFICATIONS

Units in class:	9 (I-53 to I-59 [later I-153 to I-159], I-60, I-63)
Displacement:	1,800 tons (1,633 tonnes) surfaced; 2,300 tons (2,087 tonnes) submerged
Dimensions:	Length 330ft (100m); I-56, I-57, I-59, I-60, I-63: 331ft 4in. (101m) Beam 26ft (8m) Draft 15ft 9in. (4.8m); I-56, I-57, I-59, I-60, I-63: 16ft (4.9m)
Machinery:	Two diesels with 6,800shp driving two shafts; electric motors with 1,800shp
Speed:	20kt (37km/h) surfaced; 8kt (14.8km/h) submerged
Range:	10,000nm at 10kt (18,520km at 18.5km/h) surfaced; 90nm at 3kt (166.7km at 5.6km/h) submerged
Operating depth:	200ft (61m)
Crew:	60

KD4 Type

These boats were slightly smaller than the KD3A/B, but otherwise were very similar. The number of torpedo tubes was reduced. One boat was completed in 1929 and the other two in 1930.

Armament: Six 21-in. torpedo tubes (four bow and two stern) and 14 torpedoes; one 4.7-in. deck gun. No aircraft facilities were fitted. In 1945, I-162 had her deck gun removed and was fitted for five *kaiten*.

War service: I-61 was lost before the war by collision in October 1941. I-162 spent most of her career in the Dutch East Indies and the Indian Ocean and had success sinking five ships and damaging five more. She returned to home waters in early 1944 where she remained until the war's end. I-164 also experienced success in the Indian Ocean, sinking five ships early in the war. She was sunk by a US submarine off Japan in May 1942.

KD4 TYPE SPECIFICATIONS

Units in class:	3 (I-61, I-62 [later I-162], I-64 [later I-164])
Displacement:	1,720 tons (1,560 tonnes) surfaced; 2,300 tons (2,087 tonnes) submerged
Dimensions:	Length 320ft 6in. (97.7m); Beam 25ft 6in. (7.8m); Draft 15ft 9in. (4.8m)
Machinery:	Two diesels with 6,000shp driving two shafts; electric motors with 1,800shp
Speed:	20kt (37km/h) surfaced; 8.5kt (15.7km/h) submerged
Range:	10,800nm at 10kt (20,005km at 18.5km/h) surfaced; 60nm at 3kt (111km at 5.6km/h) submerged
Operating depth:	200ft (61m)
Crew:	60

KD5 Type

These boats had essentially the same dimensions as the KD4 class, but were slightly heavier due to greater structural strength, which translated into a greater diving depth. All were completed in 1932.

Armament: Six 21-in. bow torpedo tubes and 14 torpedoes; this class introduced the 3.9-in. antiaircraft gun, and a 13mm machine gun was added to the aft end of the sail. No aircraft facilities were fitted. In 1945, I-165 had her deck gun removed and she was fitted to carry two *kaiten*.

War service: I-67 was lost before the war. On her second war cruise in the Indian Ocean, I-165 sank two ships, followed by three more on her next cruise. After participating in the Midway operation, she returned to the Indian Ocean to sink another five ships, massacring the survivors of one by machine-gun fire. After being converted to carry *kaiten*, she was sunk in 1945 off the Marianas by air attack. I-166 had a similar career, operating primarily in the Indian Ocean, where she sank six merchants. She was the first Japanese submarine to sink another submarine, when in December 1941 she sank a Dutch vessel off Borneo. She survived until July 1944 when a British submarine torpedoed her in the Strait of Malacca.

KD5 TYPE SPECIFICATIONS

Units in class:	3 (I-65 [later I-165], I-66 [later I-166], I-67)
Displacement:	1,705 tons (1,547 tonnes) surfaced; 2,330 tons (2,118 tonnes) submerged
Dimensions:	Length 320ft 6in. (97.7m); Beam 26ft 9in. (8.2m); Draft 15ft 6in. (4.7m)
Machinery:	Two diesels with 6,000shp driving two shafts; electric motors with 1,800shp
Speed:	20.5kt (38km/h) surfaced; 8.25kt (15.3km/h) submerged
Range:	10,000nm at 10kt (18,520km at 18.5km/h) surfaced; 60nm at 3kt (111.1km at 5.6km/h) submerged
Operating depth:	230ft (70m)
Crew:	75

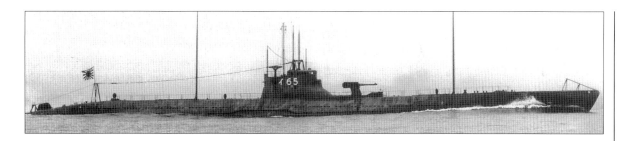

KD6A/B Types

Longer and fitted with more powerful diesels, these boats could achieve 23 knots (42.6km/h) surfaced, the highest surface speed of any submarine in the mid-1930s. The KD6B variant was slightly longer and weighed some 25 extra tons (nearly 23 tonnes), which provided an increased diving depth to 278ft (84.8m). All eight boats were completed between 1934 and 1938. In 1942–43, I-172 and apparently I-171 and I-174 were converted into cargo carriers by removing the deck gun and a number of torpedo reloads. At least I-172 could carry a 46ft (14m) *daihatsu* landing craft in addition to internal and deck cargo.

Armament: Six 21-in. bow torpedo tubes and 14 torpedoes. The first three boats carried the 3-in. gun; the last five mounted a 4.7-in. deck gun. All boats were also equipped with a 13mm machine gun (except I-174 and I-175, which mounted two).

War service: This class scored some major successes, but the loss of all eight boats showed the futility of using large submarines to attack heavily defended US fleet targets. All eight units were deployed to support the Pearl Harbor operation, where I-70 became the first Japanese submarine lost during the war, on December 10, when she was bombed by carrier aircraft. The class was also active during the Midway operation, when I-168 scored the biggest Japanese submarine success of the war when she torpedoed and sank the already damaged fleet carrier USS *Yorktown* (CV-5), and a destroyer off Midway on June 6. Later, the KD6 boats participated in the evacuation of Kiska and supply missions in the Solomons. I-175 scored the other major KD6 success when she responded to the US invasion of the Gilbert Islands in November 1943

KD6A/B TYPE SPECIFICATIONS

Units in class:	8 (KDB6A: I-68 [later I-168], I-69 [later I-169], I-70, I-71 [later I-171], I-72 [later I-172], I-73; KD6B: I-74 [later I-174], I-75 [later I-175])
Displacement:	1,785 tons (1,619 tonnes) surfaced; 2,440 tons (2,214 tonnes) submerged
Dimensions:	Length 343ft 6in. (104.7m); KD6B 344ft 6in. (105m) Beam 27ft (8.2m) Draft 15ft (4.6m)
Machinery:	Two diesels with 9,000shp driving two shafts; electric motors with 1,800shp
Speed:	23kt (42.6km/h) surfaced; 8.25kt (15.3km/h) submerged
Range:	14,000nm at 10kt (25,928km at 18.5km/h) surfaced (KD6B 10,000nm at 16kt [18,520km at 29.6km/h]); 65nm at 3kt (120.3km at 5.6km/h) submerged
Operating depth:	245ft (74m)
Crew:	70

and sank the escort carrier USS *Liscome Bay* (CVE-56). Other ships sunk by this class included a fleet oiler and five merchants. I-172 and I-173 were 1942 losses to unknown causes and a US submarine, respectively. I-168 was lost to US submarine attack in 1943. The final four boats were lost in 1944, two to surface forces and one to air attack, while I-169 was lost in a diving accident at Truk.

KD7 Type

This class was the ultimate development of the *kaidai* type and was the largest single class of its type. They were essentially repeats of the KD6 Type with less surface range. Ordered in 1939, the first boat did not enter service until August 1942 and the last was not completed until September 1943. Ten additional boats requested in the 1942 building program were canceled. In 1942–43, I-176, I-177, and I-181 were converted for cargo duty with the removal of the forward deck gun and the addition of fittings for a 46ft (14m) *daihatsu*.

Armament: Six 21-in. bow torpedo tubes and 12 torpedoes. Originally, the class was to carry two dual 25mm antiaircraft mounts, but a 4.7-in. deck gun replaced one of these mounts fitted forward of the conning tower.

War service: The fate of this class clearly demonstrated the misuse of the Imperial Navy's submarine force and its difficulty in mounting successful attacks during the late war period in the face of increasingly effective US antisubmarine defenses. Seven of the ten boats were sunk within a year of being commissioned and when I-177 was destroyed in October 1944, the entire class was removed from the Imperial Navy's order of battle. In return, the class sank only five merchants, a hospital ship, and one US submarine (the only time during the war that a Japanese submarine sank a US submarine). The most successful boat was I-176, which damaged the heavy cruiser USS *Chester* (CA-27) in October 1942 and sank the submarine USS *Corvina* (SS-226) in November 1943. I-180 sank three merchant ships. However, six of the boats scored no successes and several never even launched an attack. Of the ten boats lost, six were sunk by destroyers, two by air attack, one by US submarines, and the unfortunate I-179 was sunk in a training accident after being in service for less than one month. Many boats of this class spent much of their operational lives performing supply missions.

The final development of the KD Type was the KD7. Unlike their KD sisters, the KD7s were only medium-range submarines. After serving unsuccessfully as an attack submarine, I-176, shown here, was converted to the transport role by the removal of her 4.7-in. gun and the addition of fittings for a landing craft. (Kure Maritime Museum)

KD7 TYPE SPECIFICATIONS

Units in class:	10 (I-76 to I-85 [later I-176 to I-185])
Displacement:	1,833 tons (1,663 tonnes) surfaced; 2,602 tons (2,360 tonnes) submerged
Dimensions:	Length 346ft (105.5m); Beam 27ft (8.2m); Draft 15ft (4.57m)
Machinery:	Two diesels with 8,000shp driving two shafts; electric motors with 1,800shp
Speed:	23kt (42.6km/h) surfaced; 8kt (14.8km/h) submerged
Range:	8,000nm at 16kt (14,816km at 29.6km/h) surfaced; 50nm at 5kt (92.6km at 9.26km/h) submerged
Operating depth:	265ft (60m)
Crew:	86

A1/2 Type

The first boat in this class was laid down in January 1939. A Type submarines were intended to act as headquarters boats to coordinate the operations of submarine squadrons. This was the embodiment of the Imperial Navy's doctrine to operate its submarine forces in conjunction with the main fleet. The class was based on the J3 Type, but was provided with additional personnel accommodations and spaces for the command staff and special communications equipment. As in the J3 class, aircraft-handling facilities were provided, but the A1 class moved the catapult forward of the conning tower and faired the hangar into the sail. This much reduced the time required to prepare the aircraft for launch, and for recovery and stowage. Extra fuel and storage capacity provided this class with a patrol duration of up to 90 days. The first two boats in the class were completed before the start of the war; I-11 was not completed until May 1942. Two additional boats were ordered in the 1942 program but were canceled before construction began. The A2 Type differed from the A1 by the installation of a much less powerful diesel. This resulted in a lower surface speed but, with the additional fuel carried, a longer range. The single A2 boat was laid down in November 1942, but not completed until May 1944.

I-9 photographed during the war in what appears to be an overall black or dark gray color scheme. Note the two white bands forward for aerial recognition and the additional symbol aft of a red triangle on a white square. I-9 was lost with all hands on June 13, 1943 off Kiska Island to destroyer USS *Frazier* (DD-607). (*Ships of the World* magazine)

Armament: Six 21-in. bow torpedo tubes and 18 torpedoes; one 5.5-in. deck gun mounted aft; two twin 25mm antiaircraft guns fitted on the sail. The hangar had room for one floatplane.

War service: The A1 boats were used extensively in their intended role as submarine squadron command ships. Both I-9 and I-10 were deployed off the Hawaiian Islands at the start of the war, but the only success was I-10's sinking of a freighter. I-9's E14Y1 floatplane was used to reconnoiter Pearl Harbor on February 24, 1942 and later the aircraft also surveyed Kiska Island in the Aleutians. I-9 was lost off Kiska in June 1943 to US destroyers without sinking a single ship. I-10 went on from her Pearl Harbor deployment to have a long service life. She sank another 15 merchant ships, mainly in the Indian Ocean, where she also made extensive use of her floatplane, which flew missions over four ports in South Africa in May 1942 and over Diego Suarez in Madagascar. The latter mission set up an attack by Japanese midget submarines on a British battleship in the port. By July 1944, I-10 was committed in the Japanese effort to defend the Marianas, where she was sunk by US destroyers. I-11's first war patrol was off Australia, where she sank three freighters. In July 1943, she torpedoed and damaged the Australian light cruiser HMAS *Hobart* in the Solomons. In March 1944, she was lost to unknown causes in the area of Ellice Island. I-12 had a short, unproductive career. Her only patrol was directed against US shipping between the US West Coast and Hawaii. She sank one freighter, machine gunning the survivors, before being lost to unknown causes in January 1945 north of the Marshall Islands.

A1/2 TYPE SPECIFICATIONS	
Units in class:	4 (A1: I-9 to I-11; A2: I-12)
Displacement:	2,919 tons (2,648 tonnes) surfaced (A2 2,934 tons [2,662 tonnes]); 4,149 tons (3,674 tonnes) submerged (A2 4,172 tons [3,785 tonnes])
Dimensions:	Length 372ft 9in. (113.7m); Beam 31ft 4in. (9.5m); Draft 17ft 6in. (5.3m)
Machinery:	Two diesels with 12,400shp (A2 4,700shp) driving two shafts; electric motors with 2,400shp (A2 1,200shp)
Speed:	23.5kt (43.5km/h) surfaced (A2 18kt [33.3km/h]); 8kt (14.8km/h) submerged (A2 6.25kt [11.6km/h])
Range:	16,000nm at 16kt (29,632km at 29.6km/h) surfaced (A2 22,000nm [40,744km]); 90nm at 3kt (166.7km at 5.6km/h) submerged (A2 70nm [130km])
Operating depth:	330ft (100m)
Crew:	100

AM Type

This type was originally to be a repeat of the A2 command submarine, but during construction it was modified to serve as an aircraft-carrying submarine. Unlike previous classes, which had aircraft-handling facilities for scouting, these boats could handle two submarine-launched bomber aircraft. In this role, it was intended that they would supplement the even larger STo class. Four units were laid down; two were completed between December 1944 and March 1945, while the two others were almost complete by 1945 when construction was stopped in favor of smaller submarines for defense of the homeland. Three additional units were canceled. The AM ships were the same length as the A2 units, but with a much wider beam. This permitted the aircraft hangar to be enlarged to

I-14 after the war in US Navy hands. This class can be distinguished from the larger but similar I-400 class by the two 25mm triple mounts on the conning tower (I-400 boats had three). The top of the conning tower is offset to port, creating enough space in the hangar for two floatplane bomber aircraft. (*Ships of the World* magazine)

accommodate two of the larger Seiran aircraft. The catapult remained forward of the conning tower, but the hangar was offset to starboard and the top of the conning tower was offset to port to compensate. Both boats were fitted with a primitive form of snorkel upon completion which proved unsatisfactory in service. The range of the class was extraordinary, as required by its intended mission of striking targets in the US.

Armament: Six 21-in. bow torpedo tubes and 12 torpedoes; one 5.5-in. deck gun mounted aft; two triple and one single 25mm antiaircraft guns fitted on the conning tower. The hangar had room for two floatplanes.

War service: Having expended considerable resources on this class and the I-400s, the Navy General Staff was indecisive in finding a target for them. Originally, proposals for San Francisco, Panama, and even New York and Washington were considered, but by March 1945 it was decided to use the aircraft-carrying submarine force against the Gatun Locks of the Panama Canal. This would, it was hoped, stem the flow of reinforcements from the now inactive European Theater into the Pacific. By June 1945, however, the target was changed to the US Navy's fleet anchorage at Ulithi, the western Pacific base of the US Fast Carrier Force. The new plan, Operation *Arashi* (Mountain Storm), called for I-13 and I-14 to carry crated C6N2 "Myrt" long-range reconnaissance aircraft to Truk in order to reconnoiter Ulithi. Target information could then be relayed to the Seiran strike aircraft on the I-400 boats. I-13 left Japan for Truk on July 11, 1945 and was sunk en route by a US aircraft and destroyer attack. I-14 departed for Truk on July 14, arriving on August 4, where she unloaded her two C6N2 aircraft. After the Japanese surrender on August 15, I-14 surrendered at sea to the US Navy. The boat was later taken to Pearl Harbor, where she was sunk as a target in May 1946.

AM TYPE SPECIFICATIONS

Units in class:	2 (I-13, I-14)
Displacement:	3,603 tons (3,269 tonnes) surfaced; 4,792 tons (4,347 tonnes) submerged
Dimensions:	Length 372ft 9in. (113.7m); Beam 38ft 6in. (11.7m); Beam 38ft 6in. (11.7m)
Machinery:	Two diesels with 4,400shp driving two shafts; electric motors with 600shp
Speed:	16.75kt (31km/h) surfaced; 5.5kt (10.2km/h) submerged
Range:	21,000nm at 16kt (38,892km at 29.6km/h) surfaced; 60nm at 3kt (111km at 5.6km/h) submerged
Operating depth:	330ft (100m)
Crew:	108

B1 Type

The B Type units were conceived as long-range scouting units. The actual B1 design was developed from the KD6 Type. The B Type units retained the same aircraft-handling facilities as found on the A1 Type. On the B1, the aircraft hangar was again streamlined into the conning tower and a catapult fitted forward (one unit, I-17, had the hangar and catapult fitted aft of the conning tower). The improved streamlining resulted in a better underwater performance.

A total of 20 B1 boats was ordered in the 1939 program. The first was completed in September 1940 and the last in April 1943. This was the largest single class of fleet boats built for the Imperial Navy. This class combined the features of the *kaidai* and *junsen* types into a single hull.

Armament: Six 21-in. bow torpedo tubes and 17 torpedoes; one 5.5-in. deck gun mounted aft; one twin 25mm antiaircraft gun fitted on the conning tower. This was increased on some units to two and even three twin mounts. Units that arrived in France (I-29 and I-30) were fitted with German 37mm and 20mm quad mounts for their return voyage. The hangar had room for one floatplane. Later in the war, as floatplane operations became too dangerous, several B1 units had their hangar and catapult removed and a second 5.5-in. gun was fitted forward of the conning tower. In late 1944, I-36 and I-37 had their aircraft-handling equipment and their aft deck gun removed in order to carry four *kaiten*. Later, I-36 was again modified to carry six *kaiten*. Units fitted with *kaiten* also had a second twin 25mm gun added forward of the conning tower.

War service: This class saw extensive service during the war, being active off the US West Coast (shelling targets and launching the only air attack of the war on the continental US), in the Aleutians, in the South Pacific (often on supply missions), and in the Indian Ocean where it was successful against shipping. Losses were heavy – only I-36 survived; three

B1 Type I-26 was completed in November 1941. Note the streamlined hangar forward of the conning tower. Mounted atop the conning tower is a 25mm dual antiaircraft gun. The 5.5-in. gun was fitted aft under the radio antennae. I-26 accounted for a US Navy light cruiser before being lost to an unknown operational cause off Leyte Island in October 1944. (Kure Maritime Museum)

were sunk in 1942, nine in 1943, and seven in 1944. Eleven of the class were lost to surface attack; three were lost to Allied submarines, two to air attack, one to mines, one for operational reasons, and one for unknown reasons.

In return, B1 Type boats did enjoy some success, sinking 50 merchant or auxiliary ships and damaging another 13. As was usually the case, most ships sunk were claimed in the Indian Ocean where defenses were less intense. The star B1 performers included I-26, which damaged USS *Saratoga* (CV-3) in August 1942, putting her out of action for several crucial months during the Guadalcanal campaign; I-26 followed this up by sinking light cruiser USS *Juneau* (CLAA-52) in October. The most amazing performance was recorded by I-19 on September 15, 1942, when a single salvo of six torpedoes sank the carrier USS *Wasp* (CV-7), damaged the battleship USS *North Carolina* (BB-55), and sank a destroyer. I-25 sank a Soviet submarine and I-21 destroyed 11 merchant ships. Three boats of the class, I-26, I-27, and I-37, were involved in incidents against surviving crew members of sunken merchant ships. Three of the boats were sent on missions to carry high-priority cargo to Europe. Two of the boats, I-36 and I-37, survived late enough into the war to be fitted with *kaiten*, and used them operationally.

B1 TYPE SPECIFICATIONS

Units in class:	20 (I-15, I-17, I-19, I-21, I-23, I-25 to I-39)
Displacement:	2,584 tons (2,344 tonnes) surfaced; 3,654 tons (3,315 tonnes) submerged
Dimensions:	Length 356ft 6in. (108.7m); Beam 30ft 6in. (9.3m); Beam 30ft 6in. (9.3m)
Machinery:	Two diesels with 12,400shp driving two shafts; electric motors with 2,000shp
Speed:	23.5kt (43.5km/h) surfaced; 8kt (14.8km/h) submerged
Range:	14,000nm at 16kt (25,928km at 29.6km/h) surfaced; 96nm at 3kt (177.8km at 5.6km/h) submerged
Operating depth:	330ft (100m)
Crew:	94

B2 Type

The B2 Type units were essentially a repeat of the B1 class, but were slightly larger. The diesels fitted were marginally less powerful, but this resulted in no degradation of performance. Five of the six units in the class entered service during the second half of 1943. Another eight units planned for the 1942 program were canceled.

Armament: Six 21-in. bow torpedo tubes and 17 torpedoes; one 5.5-in. deck gun mounted aft; one twin 25mm antiaircraft gun fitted on the conning tower. The hangar had room for one floatplane. As on B1 units, some B2 boats had their hangar and catapult removed and a second 5.5-in. gun fitted forward of the conning tower. In late 1944, I-44 had her aircraft-handling equipment and aft deck gun removed in order to carry six *kaiten*.

War service: Entering the war in the face of well-developed US antisubmarine defenses and sent against fleet targets, this class achieved very little. I-41 achieved the only success, damaging the light cruiser USS *Reno* (CL-96) in November 1944. Three units were sunk by US destroyers (I-41, I-45, and possibly I-40) and two units by US submarines (I-42 and I-43), while the last unit (I-44) was sunk by acoustic torpedoes from US aircraft during a *kaiten* mission in April 1945.

The B2 Type was externally identical to the B1 Type. The last B2, I-44, shown here, was completed on January 31, 1944. The hangar, catapult, and deck gun were later removed during I-44's conversion into a *kaiten* carrier. (Kure Maritime Museum)

B2 TYPE SPECIFICATIONS	
Units in class:	6 (I-40 to I-45)
Displacement:	2,624 tons (2,380 tonnes) surfaced; 3,700 tons (3,357 tonnes) submerged
Dimensions:	Length 356ft 6in. (108.7m); Beam 30ft 6in. (9.3m); Draft 17ft (5.2m)
Machinery:	Two diesels with 11,000shp driving two shafts; electric motors with 2,000shp
Speed:	23.5kt (43.5km/h) surfaced; 8kt (14.8km/h) submerged
Range:	14,000nm at 16kt (25,928km at 29.6km/h) surfaced; 96nm at 3kt (178km at 5.6km/h) submerged
Operating depth:	330ft (100m)
Crew:	100

B3/4 Types

The three units of this class were not completed until March, June, and September 1944. Four other planned units were canceled in 1943. The B3 Type was dimensionally identical to the B2 class. The primary difference was the less powerful machinery fitted in the B3 Type, resulting in decreased surface speed. However, the B3's range was increased due to a greater fuel bunkerage. These boats were fitted from completion with a Type 22 radar fitted on top of the seaplane hangar as well as snorkels. The B4 variant was planned but never laid down. These eight boats would have been larger, with a surface speed of 22.5 knots (41.7km/h), carrying eight torpedo tubes with 23 torpedoes.

Armament: Six 21-in. bow torpedo tubes and 19 torpedoes; one 5.5-in. deck gun mounted aft; one twin 25mm antiaircraft gun fitted on the conning tower. The hangar had room for one floatplane. As on B1 and B2 boats, I-56 and I-58 had their hangar, catapult, and 5.5-in. gun

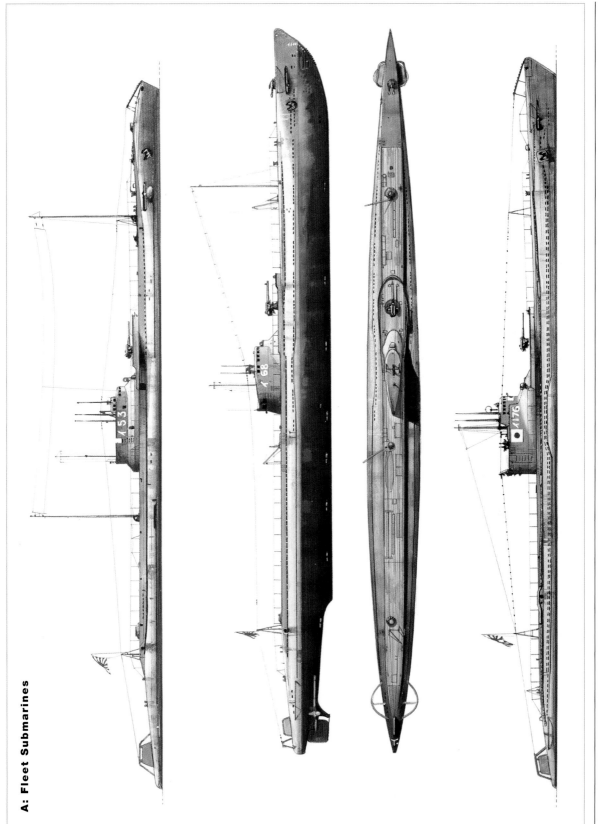

A: Fleet Submarines

A

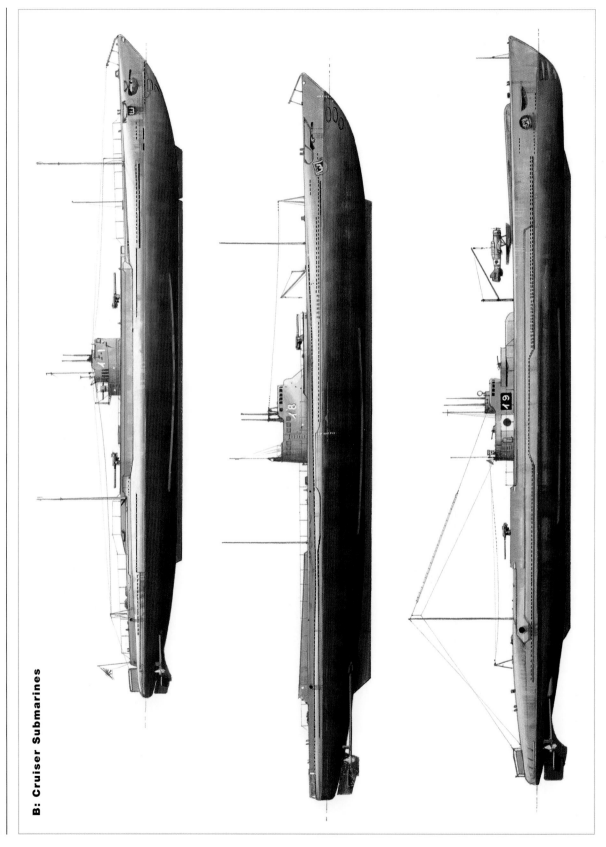

B: Cruiser Submarines

B

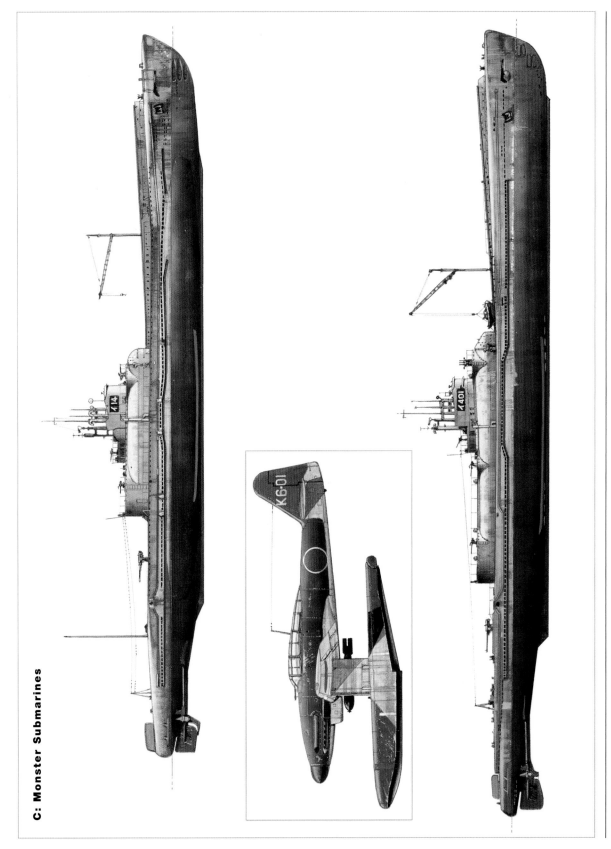

C: Monster Submarines

D: THE B1 TYPE

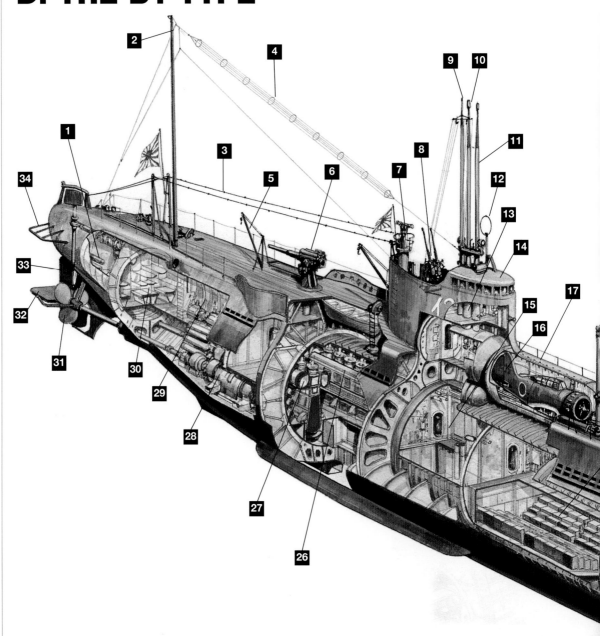

1 Air accumulators
2 Radio mast
3 Radio wire
4 Long-wave radio wire
5 Collapsible cranes for loading supplies
6 11th Year Type 5.5 in. deck gun
7 Range finder for deck gun
8 Type 96 dual 25mm antiaircraft gun
9 Signal mast
10 Number 2 periscope
11 Number 1 periscope
12 Radio direction loop
13 Navigation bridge (surface only)
14 Conning tower
15 Command post
16 E14Y1 Submarine Reconnaissance Seaplane
   in stowed condition
17 Hangar
18 Collapsible aircraft crane
19 Battery room
20 Outer hull
21 Pressure hull
22 Torpedo room (also served as crew berthing and
   mess area)
23 Aircraft catapult
24 Forward diving planes
25 Torpedo tubes
26 Main machinery room
27 Turbofan
28 Electrical motor room with main electric motors
29 Auxiliary generator room with pneumatic air pumps
30 Crew compartment
31 Screw
32 Rear diving plane
33 Rudder
34 Guard for dive plane and screw

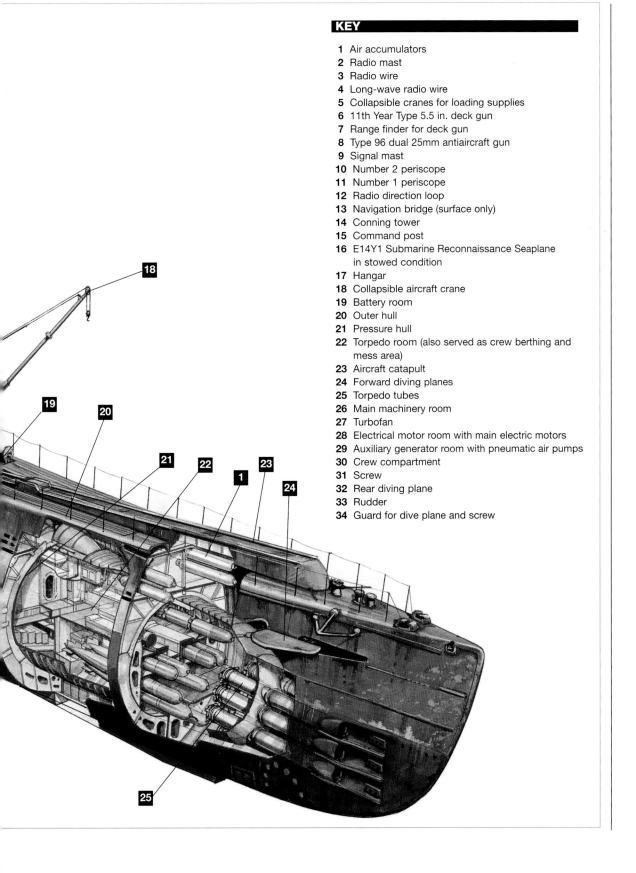

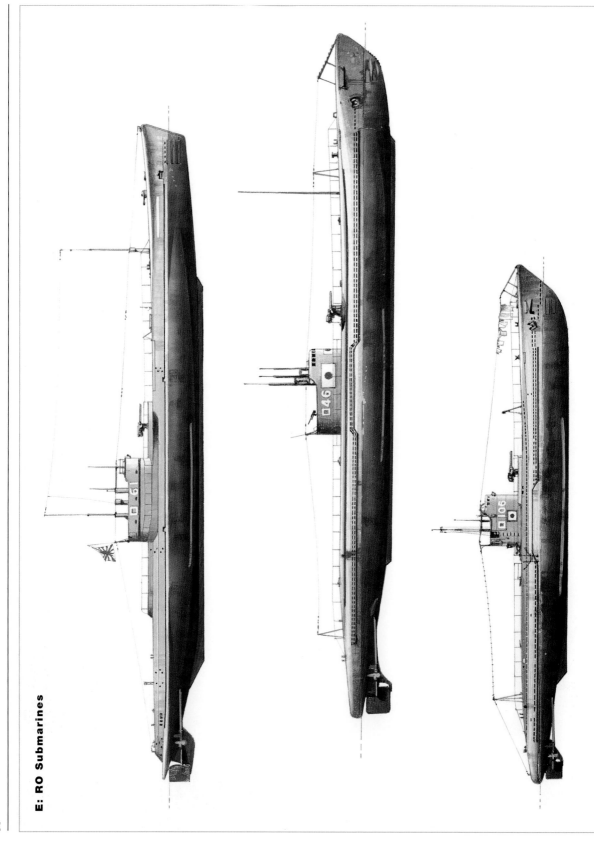

E: RO Submarines

F: Japan attacks US mainland

F

removed in 1945 to provide for the fitting of four *kaiten*. Later I-58 was modified to carry six *kaiten*.

War service: Two of the B3 units were lost without inflicting any damage on the enemy. I-54 responded to the US invasion of Leyte and was sunk by US destroyers on October 28, 1944. I-56 survived to be converted into a *kaiten* carrier and was lost in April 1945 off Okinawa. I-58 was a prime player in one of the most controversial episodes in US naval history. On July 30, 1945, she sank USS *Indianapolis* (CA-35) with three Type 95 torpedoes. Because the cruiser was not zig-zagging, its captain was held culpable for the ship's loss. With the help of I-58's skipper, his name was finally cleared in 2000. I-58 survived the war to be scuttled in April 1946.

B3/4 TYPE SPECIFICATIONS	
Units in class:	3 (I-54, I-56, I-58)
Displacement:	2,607 tons (2,365 tonnes) surfaced; 3,688 tons (3,346 tonnes) submerged
Dimensions:	Length 356ft 6in. (108.7m); Beam 30ft 6in. (9.3m); Draft 17ft (5.2m)
Machinery:	Two diesels with 4,700shp driving two shafts; electric motors with 1,200shp
Speed:	17.75kt (32.9km/h) surfaced; 6.5kt (12km/h) submerged
Range:	21,000nm at 16kt (31,892km at 29.6km/h) surfaced; 105nm at 3kt (195km at 5.6km/h) submerged
Operating depth:	330ft (100m)
Crew:	94

C1 Type

The units of the C class were intended as attack boats to operate with A Type command boats and B Type scout submarines. Their design was based on the KD6 with the increase of two torpedo tubes to provide maximum firepower. The eight forward tubes were arranged in two forward torpedo rooms, one above the other. The C1 boats were also more maneuverable underwater than the KD6. The first ship was laid down in September 1937 and the boats entered service between March 1940 and October 1941.

Armament: Eight 21-in. bow torpedo tubes and 20 torpedoes; one 5.5-in. deck gun mounted aft; one twin 25mm antiaircraft gun fitted on the conning tower. No aircraft were carried. Each boat was provided with fittings aft of the conning tower to carry one Type A midget submarine. In early 1943, I-16 was modified for duties as a supply submarine. The forward 5.5-in. gun was removed, the number of torpedo reloads was reduced, and fittings were provided aft for a *daihatsu*.

War service: This class was very active during the war and made extensive use of its ability to carry midget submarines. All five units were engaged in the attack on Pearl Harbor, with each carrying a midget sub.

I-16, I-18, and I-20 were deployed in the Indian Ocean, where they used their midget submarines to attack British shipping in Diego Suarez. The attack heavily damaged battleship *Ramillies* and sank a tanker. The boats later sank 14 freighters in the Indian Ocean as commerce raiders. Later, I-16 and I-20 each launched three more midget attacks off Guadalcanal; only a single US Navy transport was damaged. While being used as supply submarines, I-18 was sunk in February 1943 and I-16 in June 1944, both by US destroyers. I-20 was also sunk in the Solomons by US destroyers in September 1943. I-22 and I-24 were used to ferry midget submarines to attack Sydney, Australia in May 1942. The attack was a failure, sinking only an old accommodation ferry. I-22 was reported missing in the Eastern Solomons in October 1942. After the attack on Sydney, I-24 sank a freighter. I-24 was also used to launch two midget attacks on Guadalcanal and was later used for supply missions in the Solomons. In June 1943, the 2,500-ton (2,268-tonne) submarine was rammed and sunk off the Aleutians by a 675-ton (613-tonne) sub-chaser.

The C1 Type was developed from the KD6. I-18, shown here, was completed on January 31, 1941. The space aft of the conning tower was reserved for the fitting of a 46-ton (42-tonne) Type A midget submarine. (Kure Maritime Museum)

C1 TYPE SPECIFICATIONS

Units in class:	5 (I-16, I-18, I-20, I-22, I-24)
Displacement:	2,554 tons (2,317 tonnes) surfaced; 3,561 tons (3,230 tonnes) submerged
Dimensions:	Length 358ft 6in. (109.3m); Beam 30ft (9.1m); Draft 17ft 6in. (5.3m)
Machinery:	Two diesels with 12,400shp driving two shafts; electric motors with 2,000shp
Speed:	23.5kt (43.5km/h) surfaced; 8kt (14.8km/h) submerged
Range:	14,000nm at 16kt (25,928km at 29.6km/h) surfaced; 60nm at 3kt (111km at 5.6km/h) submerged
Operating depth:	330ft (100m)
Crew:	95

I-47 at Kure after her surrender. This C2 Type submarine was the only boat of its class to survive the war. I-47 spent most of her operational life, unsuccessfully, as a *kaiten* carrier. Beyond I-47 is the B1 Type boat I-36; and beyond her the Special Type submarine I-402. (US Naval Historical Center)

C2 Type

The three units of the C2 class were identical to the C1 class with the exception that they had no provisions for carrying midget submarines. The first boat was laid down in November 1942 but the boats were not completed until February–September 1944. Another seven units were canceled before being laid down.

Armament: Eight 21-in. bow torpedo tubes and 20 torpedoes; one 5.5-in. deck gun mounted aft; one twin 25mm antiaircraft gun was fitted on the conning tower. In late 1944, I-47 and I-48 were converted into *kaiten* carriers by removing their forward 5.5-in. deck gun and adding fittings for four *kaiten*. I-47 was further modified in early 1945 to carry a total of six *kaiten*.

War service: The three units of this class enjoyed no success during the war and two were sunk for their efforts. I-46 was sunk by US destroyers in October 1944 off Leyte. After conversion into a *kaiten* carrier, I-47 made extensive use of this weapon but postwar analysis indicated that her *kaiten* did no damage. I-47 survived the war, to be scuttled in April 1946. In her first war patrol as a *kaiten* carrier, I-48 was sunk in January 1945 west of Ulithi.

C2 TYPE SPECIFICATIONS

Units in class:	3 (I-46 to I-48)
Displacement:	2,557 tons (2,320 tonnes) surfaced; 3,564 tons (3,233 tonnes) submerged
Dimensions:	Length 358ft 6in. (109.3m); Beam 29ft 9in. (9.1m); Draft 17ft 6in. (5.3m)
Machinery:	Two diesels with 12,400shp driving two shafts; electric motors with 2,000shp
Speed:	23.5kt (43.5km/h) surfaced; 8kt (14.8km/h) submerged
Range:	14,000nm at 16kt (25,928km at 29.6km/h) surfaced; 60nm at 3kt (111km at 5.6km/h) submerged
Operating depth:	330ft (100m)
Crew:	95

C3 Type boat I-53 was launched February 20, 1944, and is shown in a typical late-war configuration. A Type 22 radar is fitted and the Japanese version of a snorkel is visible above the *hinomaru*. Aft of the snorkel is the boat's 25mm dual antiaircraft gun. (Kure Maritime Museum)

C3/4 Types

Due to wartime shortages, the C3 boats were fitted with inferior machinery, which resulted in a much-reduced surface speed. However, additional fuel storage gave a greater range. The number of torpedo tubes was also reduced. The first boat was laid down in March 1942 but the class was not completed until December 1943–April 1944. Fifteen boats were programmed for the C4 Type, which was to be larger, fitted with diesels capable of 20.5 knots (38km/h) on the surface and equipped with eight torpedo tubes. These were all canceled in 1943.

Armament: Six 21-in. bow torpedo tubes and 19 torpedoes; two 5.5-in. deck guns; one twin 25mm antiaircraft gun fitted on

the conning tower. In February 1944, I-52 had her antiaircraft suite increased to three twin 25mm mounts. In 1945, I-53 was converted into a *kaiten* carrier by removing both 5.5-in. deck guns. Initially, four *kaiten* could be carried; this was later increased to six.

War service: Like the B2 units, the B3 boats enjoyed little success and only one survived the war. I-52 attempted the fifth and final transit by an Imperial Navy submarine to Europe, departing Japan in March 1944. On June 23, 1944, west of the Cape Verde Islands, she was sunk by an American air-launched acoustic torpedo. I-53 scored a noteworthy success when one of her *kaiten* sank a US Navy destroyer escort in the Philippine Sea on July 24, 1945. This was the only warship sunk by this ineffective weapon. I-53 survived the war, to be scuttled in April 1946. I-55 was sunk on her first patrol in July 1944 by US destroyers off Tainan Island in the Marianas.

C3/4 TYPE SPECIFICATIONS

Units in class:	3 (I-52, I-53, I-55)
Displacement:	2,564 tons (2,326 tonnes) surfaced; 3,644 tons (3,306 tonnes) submerged
Dimensions:	Length 356ft 6in. (108.7m); Beam 30ft 6in. (9.3m); Draft 16ft 9in. (5.1m)
Machinery:	Two diesels with 4,700shp driving two shafts; electric motors with 1,200shp
Speed:	17.75kt (32.9km/h) surfaced; 6.5kt (12km/h) submerged
Range:	21,000nm at 16kt (38,892km at 29.6km/h) surfaced; 105nm at 3kt (195km at 5.6km/h) submerged
Operating depth:	330ft (100m)
Crew:	94

SH Type

The Japanese penchant for developing specialized submarines was displayed once again in the design of the SH Type. This class was intended to support the operations of flying boats in forward areas. The boat was able to carry 365 tons (331 tonnes) of aviation gas, 11 tons (10 tonnes) of fresh water, 60 550lb (250kg) bombs and 15 aircraft torpedoes. Design began before the war, but the first unit was not laid down until May 1943. When completed in January 1945, she was useless in her intended role, and was commissioned as a submarine oil tanker. A second boat, I-352, was destroyed at Kure by bombing before completion. Four additional units were canceled.

Armament: Four 21-in. bow torpedo tubes and four torpedoes. It was planned to arm this class with 5.5-in. deck guns, but these were in short supply, so four 3-in. mortars were substituted. Antiaircraft weapons included two twin and three single 25mm guns. The number of torpedoes could be increased in lieu of aircraft torpedoes.

War service: This was the largest Japanese transport submarine completed. She completed one round trip to Singapore, returning to Japan with 132,000 gallons (499,674 liters) of aviation fuel. On her second trip she was torpedoed by a US submarine in the South China Sea en route to Japan.

SH TYPE SPECIFICATIONS

Units in class:	1 (I-351)
Displacement:	3,512 tons (3,186 tonnes) surfaced; 4,290 tons (3,892 tonnes) submerged
Dimensions:	Length 363ft 9in. (111m); Beam 33ft 6in. (10.2m); Draft 20ft (6.1m)
Machinery:	Two diesels with 3,700shp driving two shafts; electric motors with 1,200shp
Speed:	15.75kt (29.2km/h) surfaced; 6.3kt (11.7km/h) submerged
Range:	13,000nm at 14kt (24,076 at 26km/h) surfaced; 100nm at 3kt (185km at 5.6km/h) submerged
Operating depth:	300ft (100m)
Crew:	77 (plus 13 aircrew)

STo (Sen-Toku or Special Submarine) Type

This class comprised the largest Japanese submarines built during the war; in fact, they were the largest submarines ever built until the introduction of the US Navy's USS *Benjamin Franklin* (SSBN-640) class of nuclear-powered ballistic missile submarines in 1965. The class took the Japanese fascination with operating aircraft from submarines to new levels, as they were designed to operate floatplane bombers against American cities. The original design called for space for two floatplanes, but this was later enlarged to carry three. The design was mainly an enlarged version of the AM design with a similar conning tower and catapult arrangement. The double hull design was unique and featured a figure eight configuration forward which turned into a horizontal figure eight amidships. In order to carry out its mission of long-range strikes, the class had sufficient fuel for a range of 37,500nm at 14 knots (69,450km at 26km/h) – unmatched until the advent of nuclear propulsion. Patrol endurance was 90 days.

Three boats were commissioned before the end of the war. The first was laid down in January 1943 and was not completed until almost two years later. The last boat was completed just before the war's end. Work on two other boats was stopped in March 1945 and several other units were canceled before construction began.

Armament: Eight 21-in. bow torpedo tubes and 20 torpedoes; one 5.5-in. deck gun, plus one single and three triple 25mm antiaircraft guns. Three bomber floatplanes could be accommodated in the hangar.

I-401 pictured after her surrender to the US Navy. This profile shows the large combined hangar/conning tower with three 25mm triple antiaircraft guns. A 5.5-in. deck gun is fitted aft. The aircraft crane is shown in its upright position. (*Ships of the World* magazine)

I-402 photographed in Kure after the war. Note the forward catapult and the large combined conning tower/hangar. (US Naval Historical Center)

War service: Despite the considerable resources devoted to this class and a number of design innovations, these boats contributed nothing to the Japanese war effort. Two of the three units completed were committed to Operation *Arashi*. While they were en route to attack Ulithi, the war ended. I-400 surrendered on August 27 and I-401 two days later. Both were later taken to Pearl Harbor by US crews for study and were sunk as targets in May and June 1946. The third boat, I-402, saw no action before Japan's surrender and was scuttled in April 1946 off Japan.

STO (SEN-TOKU OR SPECIAL SUBMARINE) TYPE SPECIFICATIONS

Units in class:	3 (I-400 to I-402)
Displacement:	5,223 tons (4,738 tonnes) surfaced; 6,560 tons (5,951 tonnes) submerged
Dimensions:	Length 400ft 3in. (122m); Beam 39ft 4in. (12m); Draft 23ft (7m)
Machinery:	Four diesels with 7,700shp driving two shafts; electric motors with 2,400shp
Speed:	18.75kt (34.7km) surfaced; 6.5kt (12km/h) submerged
Range:	30,000nm at 16kt (55,560km at 29.6km/h) surfaced; 60nm at 3kt (111km at 5.6km/h) submerged
Operating depth:	330ft (100m)
Crew:	144

ST (Sen-Taka) Type

The heavy submarine losses suffered during the first years of the war prompted the Imperial Navy to develop submarines with high submerged speeds to negate American antisubmarine forces. From 1938–40, the Japanese had evaluated an experimental high-speed submarine designated Vessel Number 71 for cover purposes. This was a small 213-ton (193-tonne) unit that reached over 21 knots (39km/h) submerged, making her the fastest undersea craft of her day. These experiments formed the basis for the ST (high speed submarine) Type, 24 of which were ordered in the 1943–44 program.

The modern streamlined appearance of the ST Type submarine is clearly shown in this photograph of I-202. These were the fastest submarines built during World War II, surpassing the German Type XXI U-boats. (Kure Maritime Museum)

I-370 seen departing for a *kaiten* mission in 1945. The *kaiten* pilots are waving from atop their weapons. Despite their great promise, the *kaiten* proved a major disappointment. I-370 was lost to USS *Finnegan* (DE-307) south of Iwo Jima on February 26, 1945. (Kure Maritime Museum)

The key components to the ST design resulted from extensive efforts to streamline the welded hull and sail; hull fittings were recessed, and even the deck guns were on retractable mounts. The electric motors were almost twice as powerful as the diesels and 4,192 high-capacity batteries provided a burst capability of up to 19 knots (35.2km/h) submerged. These were also the deepest-diving submarines built by Japan during the war. The boats were fitted with snorkels and possessed an endurance of 30 days. The first boat was laid down in March 1944; eight units were begun, but only three were finished before the war ended. Despite extensive use of prefabrication and welding, Japanese industry proved unable to get this potentially revolutionary class of submarine into service in time to affect the war.

Armament: Four 21-in. bow torpedo tubes and ten torpedoes; two retractable single 25mm guns, one forward and one aft of the conning tower.

War service: Although commissioned on February 2, 1945, I-201 did not see operational service during the war. After the war, the boat was taken to Pearl Harbor for study and was later sunk in May 1946 during ordnance tests. I-202, also commissioned in February, was damaged by US carrier raids in July 1945. She was scuttled in Japanese waters in April 1946. I-203 was completed in May 1945 and accompanied I-201 to Pearl Harbor. In May 1946, she was expended as a target.

ST (SEN-TAKA) TYPE SPECIFICATIONS

Units in class:	3 (I-201 to I-203)
Displacement:	1,291 tons (1,171 tonnes) surfaced; 1,450 tons (1,315 tonnes) submerged
Dimensions:	Length 259ft (79m); Beam 19ft (5.8m); Draft 18ft (5.4m)
Machinery:	Two diesels with 2,750shp driving two shafts; electric motors with 5,000shp
Speed:	15.75kt (29.2km/h) surfaced; 19kt (35.2km/h) submerged
Range:	5,800nm at 16kt (10,741km at 29.6km/h) surfaced; 135nm at 3kt (250km at 5.6km/h) submerged
Operating depth:	360ft (109m)
Crew:	31

D1/2 Type

The Imperial Navy had never been happy about using its combat submarines to carry out supply missions, but felt duty-bound to do all it could to support many increasingly isolated garrisons throughout the Pacific. Aside from removing these boats from their primary missions, losses on supply missions were heavy. To release combat submarines from supply duties, work on a special transport submarine design was begun in mid-1942. The D1 class could carry 22 tons (20 tonnes) of internal cargo plus 110 troops in cargo spaces in the former torpedo room and aft of the control room. External cargo included two 42ft (12.8m) landing craft and 60 additional tons (54 tonnes) of cargo. Of the 104 units projected, only 12 were completed, all between May and November 1944. The D2 design had its range reduced, as 150 tons (136 tonnes) of fuel was now used and total cargo capacity was increased to 110 tons (100 tonnes). Only a single landing craft was carried.

Armament: The first unit completed had two 21-in. bow torpedo tubes, but these were removed after initial sea trials and were not carried in subsequent units. One 5.5-in. deck gun and two single 25mm guns were carried. In early 1945, I-361, I-363, I-366, I-367, I-368, and I-370 had their deck guns and landing craft fittings removed to permit mountings for five *kaiten* to be fitted.

War service: For the loss of nine of the 13 D1/D2 boats, the Imperial Navy gained a dismal return. These boats proved to be easy targets. Four were sunk by US submarines, two on their first mission; I-373, sunk by a US submarine on August 14, was the last Japanese submarine lost during the war. The six boats converted into *kaiten* carriers accomplished nothing; two of these were lost to air-launched acoustic torpedoes and a third to US destroyers.

I-351, the only D2 Type boat completed by the Japanese. Two twin 25mm guns are visible on the aft portion of the conning tower; forward on the conning tower are the antennae for the boat's air search radar. (*Ships of the World* magazine)

D1/2 TYPE SPECIFICATIONS

Units in class:	13 (D1: I-361 to I-372; D2: I-373)
Displacement:	1,779 tons (1,614 tonnes) surfaced (D2 1,926 tons [1,756 tonnes]); 2,215 tons (2,009 tonnes) submerged (D2 2,240 tons [2,032 tonnes])
Dimensions:	Length 248ft (75.5m) (D2 242ft 9in. [74m])
	Beam 29ft 3in. (8.9m)
	Draft 15ft 6in. (4.7m) (D2 16ft 6in. [5m])
Machinery:	Two diesels with 1,850shp driving two shafts (D2 1,750shp); electric motors with 1,200shp
Speed:	13kt (24.1km/h) surfaced; 6.5kt (12km/h) submerged
Range:	15,000nm at 10kt (27,780km at 18.5km/h) surfaced (D2 5,000nm [9,260km]); 120nm at 3kt (222km at 5.6km/h) (D2 100nm [185.2km]) submerged
Operating depth:	245ft (74m) (D2 330ft [100m])
Crew:	75 (plus up to 110 troops) (D2 60)

RO SERIES SUBMARINES

L4 Type

This was the oldest class of RO boat to see active service during the war. Older RO boats, if still in existence by 1941, were reduced to a training role only. Originally based on the British L class, the L4 boats were improved versions of the preceding L3 Type boats with two torpedo tubes added and the deck gun moved forward of the sail, a position kept on all subsequent RO boat designs.

Armament: Six bow 21-in. torpedo tubes and ten torpedoes; one 3-in. deck gun and one 13mm machine gun.

War service: Despite their age, being completed between 1923 and 1927, they were used operationally during the initial phases of the war, though only committed to secondary areas. Six of the units were engaged in the attack on Wake Island where RO-66 was lost in a collision with RO-62. Another was lost after running aground early in the war, and

RO-62 shown before the war. The number 26 indicates that the boat is assigned to Submarine Squadron 26, subordinate to the 4th Fleet. RO-62 survived the war by spending most of the war as a training boat.

two more were lost in the Aleutians when six ships in the class were committed there in 1942. The only success of the class was scored when RO-61 sank a seaplane tender in the Aleutians. In 1943, the five surviving boats were assigned to training duties. One of these was later lost to mines in the Inland Sea in 1945; four survived the war.

L4 TYPE SPECIFICATIONS

Units in class:	9 (RO-60 to RO-68)
Displacement:	996 tons (904 tonnes) surfaced; 1,322 tons (1,199 tonnes) submerged
Dimensions:	Length 250ft (76.2m); Beam 24ft 6in. (7.3m); Draft 12ft 4in. (3.7m)
Machinery:	Two diesels with 2,400shp driving two shafts; electric motors with 1,600shp
Speed:	16kt (29.6km/h) surfaced; 8kt (14.8km/h) submerged
Range:	5,500nm at 10kt (10,186km at 18.5km/h) surfaced; 80nm at 4kt (148.2km at 7.4km/h) submerged
Operating depth:	200ft (61m)
Crew:	60

K5 Type

These two units were the first medium submarines designed since the L4 Type dating from the early 1920s. They were intended to be prototypes of a medium submarine suitable for series production in wartime. With more powerful engines, they had a higher surface speed than the L4. The first unit was laid down in August 1933 and the second completed in May 1937.

Armament: Four 21-in. bow torpedo tubes and ten torpedoes; one 3-in. deck gun and one 13mm machine gun.

War service: Both units were active supporting the invasion of the Dutch East Indies and then subsequently in the New Guinea/Solomons area. RO-33 sank a small freighter in August 1942 in the Coral Sea with gunfire, then massacred the survivors in the water with machine-gun fire. Later in August, after RO-33 torpedoed another freighter (which

The two K5 Type boats were successful prototypes for the much larger K6 Type class built between 1941 and 1944. Note the 3-in. gun fitted forward of the conning tower. (Kure Maritime Museum)

survived) off Port Moresby, she was sunk by the ship's Australian destroyer escort. RO-34 inflicted slight damage to a troop transport before being sunk by US destroyers in the Solomon Islands in April 1943.

K5 TYPE SPECIFICATIONS

Units in class:	2 (RO-33, RO-34)
Displacement:	700 tons (636 tonnes) surfaced; 940 tons (855 tonnes) submerged
Dimensions:	Length 239ft 6in. (73m); Beam 22ft (6.7m); Draft 10ft 6in. (3.25m)
Machinery:	Two diesels with 3,000shp driving two shafts; electric motors with 1,200shp
Speed:	19kt (35.2km/h) surfaced; 8.25kt (15.3km/h) submerged
Range:	8,000nm at 12kt (14,816km at 22.2km/h) surfaced; 90nm at 3.5kt (166.7km at 6.5km/h) submerged
Operating depth:	245ft (74m)
Crew:	75

KS (Kaigun-Sho [small]) Type

Submarines of this class were much smaller than earlier RO boats; they were more coastal than medium submarines. The design requirement set by the Navy General Staff called for a boat capable of conducting patrols around Pacific island bases, with an endurance of 21 days and a modest range of 3,500nm (6,482km). Because of their small size, roughly comparable to the German Type VII units, they were not as vulnerable to detection by radar and sonar, could dive rapidly, and were maneuverable underwater. They were built under the 1940–41 program, with the first units being laid down in June 1941. Six were completed in 1942, ten in 1943, and two in 1944.

Armament: Four 21-in. bow torpedo tubes, each with one reload; the original plans called for a twin 25mm antiaircraft mount to be fitted but this was replaced with a 3-in. gun.

War service: KS boats saw service throughout the Pacific, from the Solomons area up to the Aleutians. Many of the patrols by these units were spent on supply runs, a questionable use given the amount of cargo that could be carried. Some units also conducted patrols in the Indian Ocean. Against the Americans, results were poor, with RO-108 sinking a destroyer and RO-103 sinking two cargo ships in convoy. Results in the Indian Ocean against less well-defended targets were somewhat better, with RO-111 sinking two merchant ships, RO-113 sinking one, and RO-110 damaging two more. Not a single ship in the class of 18 survived the war. Eleven were sunk by surface forces, including five by USS *England* (DE-635) alone, two by the submarine USS *Batfish* (SS-310), and two by aircraft. Another was mined and two more went missing.

The KS Type was designed for coastal defense. These were the smallest RO boats to serve during the war. RO-106, pictured here, was destroyed north of Kavieng Island on May 22, 1944, one of five KS boats destroyed by USS *England* (DE-635). (Kure Maritime Museum)

KS TYPE SPECIFICATIONS

Units in class:	18 (RO-100 to RO-117)
Displacement:	601 tons (545 tonnes) surfaced; 782 tons (709 tonnes) submerged
Dimensions:	Length 199ft 9in. (60.9m); Beam 19ft 6in. (6m); Draft 11ft 6in. (3.5m)
Machinery:	Two diesels with 1,000shp driving two shafts; electric motors with 760shp
Speed:	14.25kt (26.4km/h) surfaced; 8kt (14.8km/h) submerged
Range:	3,500nm at 12kt (6,482km at 22.2km/h) surfaced; 60nm at 3kt (111km at 5.6km/h) submerged
Operating depth:	245ft (74m)
Crew:	38

K6 Type

These ships were based closely on the K5 class. As almost the entire force of RO submarines was obsolete by 1940, this class was an attempt to fill the shortage of medium submarines. The first of the class was laid down in October 1941; ten were completed in 1943, with the final eight finished in 1944. The increase in size from the K5 translated into greater range as more fuel could be carried. Additionally, more powerful diesel engines were fitted and the submarine's operating depth was improved. These were the last RO boats built. Many other projected units in this class were canceled after they proved alarmingly vulnerable to US antisubmarine forces.

Armament: Four 21-in. bow torpedo tubes and ten torpedoes; no guns were originally planned, but during construction a 3-in. deck gun and a twin 25mm cannon were added. These were the first RO boats capable of firing the Type 95 torpedo.

War service: The K6 class epitomized the wartime failure of the Imperial Navy's submarine force. Despite being well designed and fairly maneuverable and generally considered to be among the best of Japanese submarine designs, all but one (RO-50) were destroyed by war's end. Of these, 13 were sunk by surface ships, two by air attack (one by an acoustic torpedo) and two went missing. In exchange, the K6 boats succeeded in sinking a single destroyer escort, an 800-ton (726-tonne) yard oiler, and possibly a tank landing ship while damaging an attack transport. Most of the units in this class never even reported attacking the enemy, an utter condemnation of the over-cautious nature of their skippers. Their dismal record showed the futility of sending submarines to attack US fleet forces and the unsuitability of using submarines to defend islands against amphibious attack.

K6 TYPE SPECIFICATIONS

Units in class:	18 (RO-35 to RO-50, RO-55, RO-56)
Displacement:	1,115 tons (1,012 tonnes) surfaced; 1,447 tons (1,313 tonnes) submerged
Dimensions:	Length 264ft (80.5m); Beam 23ft (7m); Draft 13ft 6in. (4.05m)
Machinery:	Two diesels with 4,200shp driving two shafts; electric motors with 1,200shp
Speed:	19.75kt (36.6km/h) surfaced; 8kt (14.8km/h) submerged
Range:	11,000nm at 12kt (20,372km at 22.2km/h) surfaced; 45nm at 5kt (83km at 9.26km/h) submerged
Operating depth:	265ft (80m)
Crew:	61

THE IMPERIAL NAVY'S SUBMARINE FORCE – A POST MORTEM

The performance of the Imperial Navy's submarine force fell far short of expectations during the Pacific War. Originally designed to be an adjunct in the set-piece decisive battle between battleships in the western Pacific, they were ill-suited to play a role in the carrier war which developed.

The Imperial Navy had 64 submarines available at the start of the war. Of these, only 41 were modern fleet boats, two were modern medium submarines, and 21 were obsolete. The lackluster performance of the Japanese submarine force began immediately when 27 fleet submarines deployed off Hawaii in 1941 with very disappointing results. In 1942, the Imperial Navy failed to develop a coherent submarine strategy. It was still bound up in its prewar decisive battle concept; this proved ill-considered at Midway, where the submarine force failed again to perform up to expectations. The Guadalcanal campaign during the second part of 1942 was a turning point for the submarine force. While Japanese submarines did achieve some notable successes, Japan's inability to supply garrisons demanded emergency measures and the submarine force was increasingly employed in supply missions.

For the rest of the war, the submarine force carried out various different missions, from attacking shipping off the US West Coast, to carrying midget submarines to targets in Australia and the Indian Ocean, and carrying out transport operations to Europe. However, most operations were based on ill-coordinated responses to US attacks on Japanese-held islands. This typically featured setting up a submarine picket line against advancing US forces. Most often these lines were moved elsewhere when the deployment or timing of the original line was found to be faulty. In the face of US forces equipped with radar and superior intelligence, these tactics were suicidal. Throughout the war, the missions to supply cut-off garrisons increased, as did the losses.

Japanese submarines were generally much larger than any other navy's boats. Even the C1 Type boats, smallest of the A1/B1/C1 types, were significantly larger than US fleet boats. This large size was required to fulfill their envisioned role as long-range, high-surface-speed torpedo platforms, but made them ill-suited to the type of antisubmarine war they were to experience. Being large, their diving time was excessive. Once detected, they were fairly easy to destroy because of their slow submerged

I-38 was one of the last B1 boats to be completed on January 31, 1943. She survived less than two years before being sunk by USS *Nicholas* (DD-449) south of Yap Island on November 12, 1944. She scored no successes. (Kure Maritime Museum)

speed, poor maneuverability and limited diving depths. They were also noisy underwater. To make things worse, Japanese boats were equipped with generally outdated radar and acoustic equipment. The increasing effectiveness of Allied antisubmarine measures was not appreciated by the Japanese until it was too late, partly because the Imperial Navy had neglected its own antisubmarine forces before the war and had no real idea what modern antisubmarine warfare had become.

The Japanese developed a multiplicity of designs during the war and never arrived at a standardized design adapted for mass production. During the war they added 126 submarines to their fleet, making a total of 190 used during the war. All told, 129 submarines were lost – 70 to surface forces, 19 to Allied submarines, 18 to air attack, and 22 others to unknown or various causes. In return, Japanese submarines accounted for some 185 merchant ships of just over 900,000 GRT and a paltry total of warships sunk including two carriers, two cruisers, and ten smaller warships. Comparing to the German U-boats' toll of over 2,500 merchant ships alone, this was a poor harvest. All considered, the exploits of the Imperial Navy's submarine force were among the more disappointing stories of the Pacific War.

A C2 Type boat is shown leaving Japanese waters with a load of *kaiten* human torpedoes. The *kaiten* was developed late in the war as the Japanese increasingly turned to suicide weapons to stop the American advance. The basis for the *kaiten* was a modified Type 93 torpedo with a compartment for the single crewman inserted amidships. (Kure Maritime Museum)

BIBLIOGRAPHY

Bagnasco, Erminio, *Submarines of World War Two*, Sterling Publishing Co. Inc., New York (2000)

Campbell, John, *Naval Weapons of World War Two*, Naval Institute Press, Annapolis, Maryland (2002)

Carpenter, Dorr and Norman Polmar, *Submarines of the Imperial Japanese Navy*, Naval Institute Press, Annapolis, Maryland (1986)

Evans, David C. and Mark R. Peattie, *Kaigun*, Naval Institute Press, Annapolis, Maryland (1997)

Gordon, Brian and Anthony Watts, *The Imperial Japanese Navy*, MacDonald and Co., London (1971)

Januszewski, Tadeusz, *Japanese Submarine Aircraft*, Mushroom Model Publications, Redbourn, United Kingdom (2002)

COLOR PLATE COMMENTARY

JAPANESE SUBMARINE COLOR SCHEMES

All Imperial Navy submarines were originally painted in a dark gray, typically with several markings. The hull number was carried on both sides of the conning tower, either painted on or placed on a canvas marker that could be removed to obscure the boat's identity. This was often accompanied by a representation of the Japanese national ensign. On May 6, 1942, I-8 was mistakenly bombed by a Japanese aircraft off Kwajalein Island. After this, double white bands were painted on the decks of Japanese submarines as a recognition symbol.

The Imperial Navy did not utilize a well-developed system of warship camouflage during the Pacific War, but some submarines did carry camouflage measures. The Japanese believed that darker colors were harder to spot underwater and in lower visibility; accordingly, many boats were painted in an overall black scheme at the start of the war. A variation was to paint the boat's upper surfaces black, leaving the horizontal surfaces gray. Some boats employed a disruptive camouflage pattern using unknown dark colors over the original gray. Any such camouflage was instituted by the local commander.

During the war, the effectiveness of the Imperial Navy's submarine camouflage schemes was questioned, and the use of black reviewed. The "Submarine Hull Camouflage Experiment" was carried out by units attached to the Submarine School at Kure between December 1944 and March 1945. Ten older submarines participated in the study together with reconnaissance aircraft. Using paint transferred from the Germans, the Imperial Navy tested the effectiveness of the German light gray with four other colors – the standard Japanese black and gray, and two experimental colors, No.2 and No.5.

The results indicated that black was the most ineffective while the boat was surfaced, but the most effective when submerged. The German light gray was found to be ineffective in the waters off Japan. Color No.2 (light gray with a blue-gray additive) proved the best on a surfaced submarine. However, after all this effort, it is unclear if the results of this test were applied to the Imperial Navy's surviving submarines for the last months of the war.

A: FLEET SUBMARINES

The *kaidai* (KD) Type submarines were designed as long-range fleet submarines to operate in squadrons in support of the Imperial Navy's surface forces. In order to attain the desired range and surface speed, these were large submarines, larger than those of any other World War II Navy. The top profile shows the lead unit of the KD3A Type, I-153. The KD3A/B was the first large class of KD boats to enter service. I-153 survived the war after a brief period of active service during which she scored no successes.

The middle profile shows the next large class of KD boats, the eight-unit KD6 class. These boats were longer and fitted with more powerful machinery than their predecessors, making them the ultimate development of the KD design philosophy, which emphasized range and speed. Note the deck gun fitted forward of the KD trademark faired conning tower.

The bottom profile depicts I-176, a member of the KD7 class. This class was externally identical to the KD6 class. I-176 was the most successful boat in her class. After a fairly long wartime career, she was sunk on 17 May 1944 east of New Ireland by a US destroyer.

B: CRUISER SUBMARINES

The *junsen* (cruiser) boats were designed for long-range independent operations, with emphasis on range and sea keeping. The top profile shows the J1 Type boat I-1. Her boat-like hull is obvious. No aircraft were carried, but the boat was heavily armed with two 5.5-in. guns (shown fore and aft of the conning tower) and 20 torpedoes.

The ultimate development of the *junsen* boats was the J3 Type. I-8, shown in the middle profile, retained a heavy armament in the form of a forward 5.5-in. deck gun and 20 torpedoes, and added the capability to handle aircraft. The aft-facing catapult is evident, but the twin-cylinder hangars are not visible.

A derivative of the J3 Type was the larger A1 Type. Shown in the bottom profile is I-9. These boats had their hangars integrated into their conning tower and their catapult installed forward of it. This permitted access to the hangar from within the pressure hull, making launch and recovery of the submarine's single floatplane much quicker. Also evident is the 5.5-in. deck gun and the two positions of antiaircraft guns fitted in the conning tower.

C: MONSTER SUBMARINES

The Imperial Navy was the only navy to employ attack aircraft from submarines during the Pacific War. To embark these, the Japanese designed two classes destined to be the largest submarines employed during World War II. The top profile depicts the AM Type boat I-14. The basis for the AM design was the large A2 command submarine. Note the combined hangar/conning tower, large enough for two bomber floatplanes.

Japanese submarines used different color schemes during the war. These are B1 Type boats (I-29 right and I-27 left); one has an overall black scheme while the second is in dark gray with upper portions of the conning tower and hanger painted black. Both carry the national ensign on removable canvas markers fitted on frames on the conning tower. Neither boat carries its hull number.